Life is just a Dream.... so Anything is Possible.

Victoria Capper

BookLeaf
Publishing

Presentation by *BookLeaf Publishing*

Web: www.bookleafpub.com

E-mail: info@bookleafpub.com

ISBN: 9789357442305

First edition 2023

My daughter who amazes me everyday. Also to my friends and family who know the real me and love me just the way I am.

ACKNOWLEDGEMENT

Book Leaf publishing and Facebook Advertising.

New Beginnings.

NEW BEGINNINGS

New beginnings, a time for reflection.
What's passed is past and what has not yet
come, is yet to pass.
I awake, so groggy. Sleep alluded me, yet
dreams haunted me.
The day for New beginnings has arrived.
What awaits me?

In short time another chapter ends.
I do not feel relief, I do not feel sad.
I do not feel.
I am numb.

I am in pain bit it doesn't hurt.
I am upset but I cannot cry.
I want to scream but I cannot muster sound.
I want to live but I want to die.

Today is a new beginning.

Feeling Lost.

I feel so lost although I know what to do
I have to sort my head out, I have to move.
I try to rise, to wash my face
I close my eyes, I feel a disgrace.

Trying to dress, to feel more human
Grey roots showing I'm an older woman.
Is that the problem?, I have no clue
So many don't get to do what I can do.

To sit back down and give In to the despair
Tears falling hard, like I'll never repair.
The darkness envelopes me, with no sign of
letting
Tomorrow may be brighter? I try not forgetting.

Everything is hurting me, mentally unwell
But I know how lucky I am, I can tell.
I am loved
I am liked
I'm where I'm meant to be.
I am safe
I am secure
I am okay being me.

Night terrors.

I wake with a start. My heart beats so fast I feel
it will explode through my chest.
I am warm but not bathed in sweat.
I tried to climb the wall again. As if that will
save me.
Living with this knowing I'll never be free.

My eyes are open. I do not care to sleep.
For when I sleep I remember.
What is to come. To all of us.
What is to come. The darkness.

I am shaking with fear. My stomach churning
like a machine.
For years I have felt so scared and not at peace.
But the shaking like a leaf of a tree. That is new.
Even for me.
I need it to stop I need it to let me be.

I look around the room. Hoping for safety.
But this cannot be hid from.
This is life for two decades and four
This is life until it is no more.

I don't fit in.

I am here. For you. For them. For everyone.
But I don't fit in.
I talk. I speak. I'm listened to. I advise.
But I don't fit in.
I wake to a beautiful day. I smile as birds sing.
But I don't fit in.

I move around. I do for others. I do for myself.
But I don't fit in.
I watch you. I watch them. I watch everyone.
But I don't fit in.
I laugh. I joke. I smile and dance.
But I don't fit in.

Does anyone fit in? What IS fitting in?
Moving in one direction. Forwards. Upwards.
Onwards.
I try with all my might to move with others.
But I don't fit in.

I don't know that I want to fit in.
To fit in is to be the same and I am most
definitely not the same.

I am empty.

I am empty.
Empty of love. Empty of feeling. Empty of
energy
Music, once lively in my head, Is now a dull
thud.
I wonder if I will feel the music again.

People look the same but they are acting strange.
Differently.
Crossing both white lines and boundaries.
Forever disappointing me.

I am empty.
Empty of compassion. Empty of forgiveness.
Empty of care.
Dance, once flowing through my body, is now
steadfast.
Will I ever feel light enough to dance again.

To do what I used to do seems so rare.
Stunted.
I sit and stare and think of nothing
Disappointed in myself.

I feel empty. Again.
How many times will this be?
This feeling empty, whilst alive
It's really not so good, being me.

Depression.

I'm writing deep but feel light on my feet,
The clouds are passing by.
Depression kills, I try to feel
All the good things in my life.

I do not take for granted,
The sights I see today.
The birds are singing, The sun is shining
And I'm still alive to play.

I didn't think I'd make it this time!
The clouds, they grew so dark.
I waited it out, I fought like mad
But somehow missed the mark.

I don't want to think of others,
The guilt is hard to bare.
I cry and cry, I try to stop
But why should I really care.

To feel these things, is more than enough,
For one person all alone!
But to have a lover, is a burden to carry
The guilt like a broken bone.

I know he cares, he wants to help!
But I have to do it first.
To save myself and cure this pain,
I have to take those steps.

To walk alone, to say goodbye!
To fix this pain and save my life.

Not my own.

I had a baby girl
But she wasn't mine at all.
I had to be a mummy,
For a baby not from my tummy.

I loved that baby,
Like nothing you can imagine!
I wished that baby was mine.
With her I spent all my time.

One day that baby grew up,
and had babies of her own.
And It is lovely to see,
What she has learnt from me.

That baby is my niece,
And everyone should know.
That to be a mum to a child
Is the most precious gift to own.

The truth.

Life changed drastically,
One day in late 19.
The TV lied and people died
But something didn't sit right for me.

I went about my business,
Life was normal for a while.
But then I faced the demons,
And their hatred and bile.

For thinking differently
Than what we're told to think.
Makes others mad and I feel sad,
Because, 'you've broken the link'.

I am an outsider,
Alone with the things I see.
My thoughts are crazy and mad
And the people won't let me be.

''You must tow the line and do as you're told,
Or we will never be free''.
But I know the truth. I know the score!
We will all be locked up forever more.

I have so much to say.

I have so much to say,
But I write blank.
I have so much to do,
But I move so still.

I have so much I want,
Yet to get them I don't.
I have so many places to be,
Yet nowhere I go.

I have so much love to give,
But I struggle to share it.
I have so much rage,
But I struggle to contain it.

I have such a useful mind,
Yet I fail to use it.
I have such a lovely life,
Yet I fail to live it.

Pain.

Physical pain strikes every day.
To the core of my body.
To the tips of my fingers.
To the top of my head.

It rages and burns,
And screams non stop.
It pulses and thumps,
Until I think I can't take any more.

I wonder how people live.
Do they feel the same pain?
Do they walk around free of it?
Do they even know how much I have?
Do they even care?

The 21 day writing challenge.

The end of the challenge is near.
I feel a failure,
As I always do.
But this is not true.

I am not a failure.
But this, like life.
Feels very much a scam.
Yet, I will do what I can.

I am struggling to write.
I doubt myself.
I procrastinate and time spend,
But I always succeed in the end.

So I will quicken my pace!
Let the words just tumble.
Maybe they will print it.
Maybe they will bin it.

But when I look back,
I will see my struggle.
Of the start of the year 2023
And the brain, in the life that is me.

A pact.

I will spend the rest of the year
Working hard.
To be more myself,
Less fake
And to make sure I go far.

I will travel and see the world.
I will stop worrying.
I will laugh more,
Cry less
And move less hurriedly.

I will use my time more efficiently,
To keep motivated.
To do the things I want to do
And never doubt myself.
I will feel more satiated.

My life itself is 'the' purpose.

Illness.

15

An illness can ruin your life.
Where can u go?
Can u make it?
Can you be on time?

An illness that hurts.
An illness that changes your face.
Your shape, your image
The darkness, it lurks.

Confidence shook.
Remission a dream.
Medicine taken.
Memory mistook.

Learn to live with it,
It's incurable
Don't let it beat you!
Or you'll fall deep in a pit.

My baby.

I fought for my baby
For her to exist
I paid lots of money
I paid with my emotions.
She came to be,
The most perfect baby in every way.
She grew so healthily.
She cared for others.
She was so kind and sweet.
People would cling to her.
Everyone loved her.

My baby has grown.
Into the most beautiful young person.
She's still so kind, so funny and brilliant.
I love her with every fibre of my being.

But a darkness lingers for my baby girl.
A cult. A religion. An ideology. The devil
himself.
I will not lose my baby girl to the darkness.
I will keep her in the light.
With every fibre of my being .

Time.

17

When I was a little girl
I thought I had forever.
But time goes so fast ,
Less time forward than past.

When I was a teen
I didn't appreciate life.
I wanted to grow up,
Because I didn't have much luck.

When I was an adult
I had my only child.
I was meant to be a mum
The best years of my life by far.

Now I am middle aged.
I want time to pause.
I'm not sure what comes next
But I hope I've not yet experienced the best.

Storms Pass.

The wind howls and the trees shake,
The lightning strikes.
A storm has arrived,
And the clouds are moving by.

The rain falls fast.
How I love to dance in the rain.
The thunder drums bang,
And I jump with fright.

The weather fights on,
And leaves fall at my feet.
I shudder with cold,
And I admire the row.

When a storm has gone,
The sun will shine.
Just like your life itself,
The storm will always pass.

How deep.

How deep should a poem be?
Of how my life should seem.
But as its my book,
It should be a real look,
Into the wonderful world of me.

It should be whatever I'm feeling,
But hope that not many are reading.
The gloom of my life,
With all of its strife,
The wonderful life of this being.

I thought I could write a book of poetry.
Yet it seems it's just woe of me.
Its doom and gloom,
With lots of room,
To add another two or three.

New beginnings. Again.

I'm feeling better, far from the start.
I have been writing daily, from my heart.
It is therapy for the soul, to let it all out.
Good or bad, happy or sad, to write without
doubt.

Without fear or worry, the thoughts that I feel
To speak it out loud, so loud and so clear.
To re read and to edit. To feel those feelings
again.
From the days before now, when I felt at the
end.

The bad feelings passed this time. It's finally
lifted.
I know that I am blessed, so lucky and gifted.
I started a new year with such anger and hatred,
Upset by people even though they are strangers.

I am used to depression, its my oldest mean
friend.
It has tried to kill me, but I will not make my life
end.
It overwhelms me and comes on so quick
I try and I fight. I can't find a permanent fix.

But for now, the mood has lifted. I am happy
and free.
The clouds have rolled away and I can clearly
see.
A new day awaits. A new year, new beginnings.
I awake tomorrow with hope, to see what the
day brings.

Limerick Vic.

There once was a girl called Vickie.
Who grew up incredibly icky.
She got really sick,
It was taking the mick.
So then she became really picky.

She got diagnosed with Crohns disease.
Which hurt her bones and her knees.
She had 5 ops,
And lost the plot.
Now she cant eat many peas.

But Sicky Icky Vickie,
Grew up to be rather pretty.
Pretty thick skinned,
She pretty soon binned,
Anyone she didn't find witty.

She has a really great, good life,
With hardly any real strife.
She has loved ones,
And luckily never runs,
Out of lots of fun and love in her life.

The end.

9 789357 442305